HIGH INTEREST LOW READING Level BOOKS FOR TEENS

Hi-Lo Short Stories for High School Struggling Readers | Relevant, Age-Appropriate Topics for IEP, ESL, and SPED Classrooms

DR. FANATOMY
★★★★★

copyright@ dr. fanatomy 2025

All rights reserved. No part of this publication may be reproduced, distributed, or transmitted in any form or by any means, including photocopying, recording, or other electronic or mechanical methods, without the prior written permission of the publisher, except in the case of brief quotations embodied in critical reviews and certain other noncommercial uses permitted by copyright law.

This book is a work of non-fiction, and any resemblance to actual persons, living or dead, or actual events is purely coincidental.

The information and techniques described in this book are intended for educational and informational purposes only. The author and publisher shall not be held liable for any injury, damage, or loss arising from using or misusing the information presented in this book.

While every effort has been made to ensure the accuracy of the information contained within this book, the author and publisher make no warranties or representations express or implied, about the completeness, accuracy, reliability, suitability, or availability with respect to the contents of this book for any purpose. The use of any information provided in this book is at the reader's own risk.

TABLE OF CONTENTS

INTRODUCTION: THIS BOOK GETS YOU (Pg:3-6)

- If you hate reading... This is different
- What is HI-LO Reading?
- How It Works
- Who is this for
- How to use this book
- Sneak Peek: What's Inside

CHAPTER 1: GRAMMAR WITHOUT THE GROANING (Pg:7-15)

- No red pens allowed—just smart strategies!
- Why Grammar Feels Impossible
- Myth-Buster
- HI-LO Magic = High-Interest + Low-Stress
- Grammar Hack → SWAP & SNAP
- Confidence Boost
- Warm-Up: Text-It-Like-A-Friend
- Activity Zone and Answers
- Quick-Flip Guide: 20 Fancy Words ↔ Simple Swaps

CHAPTER 2: THE WRONG CROWD (Pg:16-24)

- Learning Objectives
- Story — The Wrong Crowd
- Grammar FOCUS — Fixing Fragments
- Real Talk— Pressure VS. Power
- Character Motivation Matrix
- Chapter Summary
- Grammar + Story Integration Table: Fix the Fragments in Context
- Activity Zone and Answers

TABLE OF CONTENTS

CHAPTER 3: TEXT ME LATER (Pg: 25-33)

- Learning Objectives
- Story — Text Me Later
- Digital Drama Breakdown
- Grammar Focus — Commas in Dialogue
- Checklist: Does Your Dialogue Work?
- Reflection — Tone, Texts & Trusts
- Visual Learning Tools
- Punctuation Fixes at a Glance — Dialogue Repair Cheatsheet
- Mind Map 1: Digital Drama Flow — What Went Wrong?
- Mind Map 2: Punctuation Power — Why Commas Matter
- Chapter Summary
- Activity Zone and Answers

CHAPTER 4: LATE AGAIN (Pg: 34-41)

- Learning Objectives
- Story — Jamal's Bad Day
- Mind Map: Jamal's Morning Fix
- Grammar Focus— Run-On Sentences
- Run-On Radar: Grammar Tip Box
- Flowchart: How to Fix a Run-On
- Real Talk — Why Punctuality Matters
- Quick Write
- Activity Zone and Answers

CHAPTER 5: NO FILTER (Pg:42-49)

- Learning Objectives
- Story — Maya's Mistake
- Mind Map: Maya's Post Impact

TABLE OF CONTENTS

- Grammar Focus — Homophones: Your vs. You're
- How to Choose the Right One
- Table: Homophone Fixes in Social Media Captions
- Tip Box: Quick Homophone Check
- Real Talk — Think Before You Post
- Table: Posting With Care vs. Without
- Activity Zone and Answers

CHAPTER 6: THE GROUP PROJECT (Pg: 50-59)

- Learning Objectives
- Story — Ava's Heavy Load
- Mind Map: Ava's Group Project
- Grammar Focus — Subject-Verb Agreement
- Flowchart: Do Your Subject and Verb Agree?
- Real Talk — Sharing The Load
- Activity Zone and Answers

CHAPTER 7: FAKE IT TIL YOU BREAK IT (Pg:60-69)

- Learning Objectives
- Story — The Fake Profile Fiasco
- Mind Map: Eli's Fake Profile Journey
- Grammar Focus — Pronoun Power: He, She, They
- Table: Pronoun Corrections from the Story
- Flowchart: Choose the Right Pronoun
- Real Talk — Being Real Online
- Table: Real vs. Fake Online Behavior
- Real-Life Connection
- Activity Zone and Answers

TABLE OF CONTENTS

CHAPTER 8: LOCKER ROOM TALK (Pg:70 -77)

- Learning Objectives
- Story – The Gossip Trap
- Mind Map: Kyla's Gossip Trail
- Grammar Focus – Mastering Quotation Marks
- Punctuation Rules
- Real Talk – Breaking The Rumor Cycle
- Discussion Questions
- Activity Zone and Answers

CHAPTER 9: SECOND CHANCE (Pg:78-85)

- Learning Objectives
- Story – The Cheating Fix
- Mind Map: Rico's Cheating Trail
- Grammar Focus – Get Verb Tenses Right
- Table: "Was vs. Is: Pick the Right Time!"
- Real Talk – Choosing Honesty
- Discussion Questions
- Activity Zone and Answers

CHAPTER 10: UNFOLLOW ME (Pg:86-93)

- Learning Objectives
- Story – Breaking Free
- Mind Map: Sofia's Friendship Trail
- Grammar Focus – Mastering Contractions
- Real Talk – Spotting Toxic Friends
- Real Talk – Choosing Honesty
- Table: Friendship Check
- Activity Zone and Answers

TABLE OF CONTENTS

CONCLUSION (Pg:94-96)

APPENDIX (Pg:97-105)

- Appendix -A: Grammar Hacks Cheat Sheet
- Appendix -B: Reading Like a Pro — Mindmap Strategy
- Appendix -C: Fix Your Writing — Flowchart Strategy
- Appendix - D: Life Lessons Venn Diagram
- Appendix - E: Common Vocabulary Mistakes (And What to Say Instead)
- Appendix - F: Most Common Grammar Goofs (And How to Fix Them)
- Appendix - G: Text Slang vs. School Writing
- Appendix - H: Capitalization Rules Made Easy
- Appendix I: Quick Fix for Run-On Sentences
- Appendix - J: 10 Words That Often Confuse Teens
- Appendix - K: 10 Fast Grammar Reminders
- Appendix - L: 10 Reading Tricks That Actually Work

Introduction: This Book Gets You

High-Interest, Low-Reading-Level Books for Teens

📣 "If you hate reading... This is different."

You:

- "Books are too long."
- "Why does everything sound like a textbook?"
- "I'm just not a reader."

This book:

✔ Short stories (like scrolling TikTok, but you learn something)
✔ No fancy words ("ramifications" → "consequences")
✔ Real teen problems (social media drama, peer pressure, toxic friends)

What is HI-LO Reading?

- Build your reading fluency (so you can read faster and smoother).
- Expand your vocabulary (so you can learn new words and use them like a pro).
- Sharpen your critical thinking skills (so you can analyze, predict, and solve problems).

"High-Interest + Low Reading Level" = Stories you WANT to read that you CAN read.

How It Works:

Regular Books	Hi-Lo Books
Long paragraphs	Short lines, lots of dialogue
Formal language	Texts, slang, how you actually talk
Boring topics	Drama, mistakes, real-life messes

Example:

✗ "The pedagogical methodology was ineffective."
✅ "Her teaching didn't work."

🎯 Who is this for

Teens Who:
- Zone out after 2 pages
- Think grammar is torture
- Want stories that feel real

Teachers Who Need:
- IEP/SPED-friendly material
- Short, engaging passages for ESL students
- No-prep lessons with built-in grammar

Parents Who Want:
- Books their kid won't abandon after Chapter 1
- Stories that teach lessons (without lecturing)

How to use this book:

Rule #1: You're in charge.
- Skip around! Start with any story.
- Hate an exercise? Do every other one.

Each Chapter Gives You:
1. **A Story** (under 400 words) – Like watching a YouTube short
2. **Secret Grammar** – Hidden in the drama (no boring drills)
3. **Real Talk** – Questions that matter ("When was the last time you lied to fit in?")
4. **Quick Challenges** – Fix a text message, spot the mistake

Sneak Peek: What's Inside

Stories That Don't Suck:

- "The Wrong Crowd" – A lie gets exposed at a party
- "Text Me Later" – A screenshot ruins a friendship
- "No Filter" – When a post goes viral for the wrong reasons

Grammar You'll Use:

- How to fix run-on sentences (so your texts make sense)
- Your vs. You're (so your posts don't get roasted)
- Quotation marks (so people know who said what)

Before You Start...

You don't need to:
- Read fast
- Love grammar
- Finish every exercise

You just need to:
- Try one story
- Give yourself credit for trying
- Laugh at the drama

Ready? Let's go

Chapter 1: Grammar Without The Groaning

7

No red pens allowed—just smart strategies!

Learning Targets

- I can spot sentences that sound stiff and turn them into smooth, everyday English.
- I can replace big "SAT words" with simple, powerful words.
- I can add commas or periods where I naturally pause when reading aloud.

Why Grammar Feels Impossible

Teens Speak

- *"I freeze when I see big paragraphs."*
- *"This is low-key hard."*
- *"Why do essays sound like robot talk?"*

What's Really Going On?

😖 Feeling	🔍 Hidden Reason	💡 Quick Fix for Students	📖 Teacher / Parent Strategy
Big paragraphs	Eyes need a "rest stop"	**Chunk it!** Break into 2–3-line bites.	Model "think-aloud" chunking with a doc camera.
Fancy words	They hijack focus	**Swap it!** Trade one hard word for two easy ones.	Build a class "Swap Wall" of word pairs.
Grammar rules	Past red-pen memories	**Focus on clear, not perfect.**	Use "glow & grow" feedback—start with what works.

Myth-Buster

☒ "You need perfect grammar to understand a story."

☑ You only need clear grammar. Save "perfect" for the **style guide.**

Breathe & Break (Student Trick)

Read aloud. When you run out of breath or your voice dips → insert a comma (,) or period (.) there.

She scrolled TikTok all night, and her phone died.

HI-LO Magic = High-Interest + Low-Stress

"Hard vs. Helpful" Sentences

Hard (Brain-Freeze)	Helpful (Flow Mode)	Why It Works
The ramifications were profound.	*His choices changed everything.*	Short, concrete words
She endeavored to circumvent him.	*She tried to dodge him.*	Active verb + fewer syllables
It was an inconsequential mishap.	*It was a small oops.*	Familiar vocab + humor
They commenced their excursion at dawn.	*They started their trip at dawn.*	Uses spoken-language verb

Grammar Hack → SWAP & SNAP

- Spot any 4-plus-syllable word.
- Swap it for a 1- or 2-syllable buddy.
- Snap—meaning hits instantly!

Utilize → use | Comprehend → get

😀 Long Word (4+ Syllables)	🔄 Swap With	⚡ Snap Meaning
Utilize	Use	Get it fast
Comprehend	Get	Instantly clear
Demonstrate	Show	Easy to grasp
Facilitate	Help	Straightforward
Participate	Join	Makes sense quick
Communicate	Talk	Clear and direct
Investigate	Check	Simple to follow
Implement	Do	Gets to the point
Appreciate	Like	Quick connection
Consideration	Thought	Easy to understand

Confidence Boost

Mini-Affirmations (Post on the wall!)
1. I read to understand, not to impress.
2. Mistakes teach me—they don't break me.
3. Every page I finish = one micro-win.

Warm-Up: Text-It-Like-A-Friend

Rewrite each formal line as if texting a friend (≤12 words, emojis welcome).

📚 Formal Sentence	📱 Text-Style Rewrite
Please refrain from arriving after the bell.	Don't be late, lol 🏃
Her participation was commendable.	She totally crushed it 🙌
I am unable to attend the meeting today.	Can't make it today 😓
Your assignment was exceptionally well-written.	Your paper was 🔥
He demonstrated excellent leadership skills.	Dude was a boss 💼
Kindly submit your project by Friday.	Don't forget to send it by Fri! 📅
That behavior is not acceptable.	Not cool, bro 🚫
I appreciate your assistance with the task.	Thanks for the help! 🙏
The cafeteria will remain closed today.	No lunch line today 🍽️
The teacher is not available at the moment.	She's busy rn, try later ⏰
We will begin promptly at 9 a.m.	Starting sharp at 9 🕘
He requires additional support in mathematics.	He needs some math help 📘

ACTIVITY ZONE

ACTIVITY 1 – MATCH THE SMOOTH SENTENCE

Draw a line or write the letter to match the formal sentence with its smoother version.

Formal Sentence	Smooth Sentence
A. The precipitation intensified progressively.	1. We ate a lot.
B. They embarked upon an expedition.	2. Start reading when you can.
C. I discovered his duplicity unacceptable.	3. They went on a trip.
D. Commence reading at your earliest convenience.	4. Then the team left.
E. Subsequently, the team vacated the premises.	5. I couldn't stand his lies.
F. We consumed substantial nourishment.	6. The rain got heavier.

ACTIVITY 2 – SWAP & SNAP!

Replace the bold word with a simpler one.

1. She felt **melancholy** all day.
2. The coach gave a **motivational** speech.
3. The test was **excruciating**.
4. He showed immense **dedication** to the team.
5. That rule is **obsolete** now.
6. The results were **catastrophic**.

ACTIVITY 3 – BREATHE & BREAK

Add // Where you'd pause for a comma or period.

1. I wanted pizza but my wallet was empty.
2. The rumor spread fast nobody knew the truth.
3. He sighed he had to start over.
4. She opened the app the screen glowed bright.
5. My sister loves horror movies I don't.
6. We studied all night now we're exhausted.

ACTIVITY 4 – TEXT TRANSLATION CHALLENGE

Turn each formal line into a friendly text (≤ 10 words).

1. I apologize for my tardiness.
2. Your attendance tomorrow is mandatory.
3. We appreciate your cooperation in this endeavor.
4. The assignment is due at your earliest convenience.
5. Please refrain from disruptive behavior.
6. Kindly notify me of your decision forthwith.

ANSWERS
🎯 ACTIVITY ZONE

ACTIVITY 1 – MATCH THE SMOOTH SENTENCE

- A → 6
- B → 3
- C → 5
- D → 2
- E → 4
- F → 1

ACTIVITY 3 – BREATHE & BREAK

- I wanted pizza // but my wallet was empty.
- The rumor spread fast // nobody knew the truth.
- He sighed // he had to start over.
- She opened the app // the screen glowed bright.
- My sister loves horror movies // I don't.
- We studied all night // now we're exhausted.

ACTIVITY 2 – SWAP & SNAP!

1. She felt melancholy all day. → She felt sad all day.
2. The coach gave a motivational speech. → The coach gave an inspiring speech. (or "encouraging")
3. The test was excruciating. → The test was painful. (or "agonizing" - but "painful" is simplest)
4. He showed immense dedication to the team. → He showed great dedication to the team. (or "huge", or "tremendous")
5. That rule is obsolete now. → That rule is outdated now. (or "old-fashioned")
6. The results were catastrophic. → The results were disastrous.

ACTIVITY 4 – TEXT TRANSLATION CHALLENGE

- Sorry I'm late!
- You gotta be there tomorrow.
- Thanks for helping us!
- Turn it in ASAP.
- Don't stir up drama.
- Let me know ASAP.

QUICK-FLIP GUIDE: 20 FANCY WORDS ↔ SIMPLE SWAPS

Fancy Word	Simple Swap	Example (Fancy → Simple)
Commence	Start	*We commence now. → We start now.*
Terminate	End	*Game terminates. → Game ends.*
Utilize	Use	*Utilize a pen. → Use a pen.*
Inquire	Ask	*Inquire later. → Ask later.*
Reside	Live	*I reside here. → I live here.*
Purchase	Buy	*Purchase snacks. → Buy snacks.*
Require	Need	*I require help. → I need help.*
Assist	Help	*Assist me! → Help me!*
Consequently	So	*Consequently, I left. → So I left.*
Sufficient	Enough	*Not sufficient. → Not enough.*
Approximately	About	*Approximately 5. → About 5.*
Numerous	Many	*Numerous apps. → Many apps.*
Facilitate	Help / Ease	*Facilitate learning. → Help learning.*
Inevitable	Unavoidable / Sure	*Inevitable win. → Sure win.*
Perplexed	Confused	*I'm perplexed. → I'm confused.*
Ameliorate	Improve	*Ameliorate grades. → Improve grades.*
Expedite	Speed up	*Expedite the process. → Speed it up.*
Benevolent	Kind	*Benevolent teacher. → Kind teacher.*
Cognizant	Aware	*Be cognizant. → Be aware.*
Persevere	Keep going	*Persevere! → Keep going!*

Chapter 2 : THE WRONG CROWD

CHAPTER 2 – THE WRONG CROWD

Learning Objectives:

☑ I can spot peer-pressure tactics in text conversations
☑ I can find and fix sentence fragments
☑ I can map short-term vs. long-term consequences
☑ I can prove I understand story details

STORY — THE WRONG CROWD

(Text message format + inner thoughts)

📱 **8:03 a.m. — GROUP CHAT**
ZAK: Skip 4th. Arcade tournament TODAY 🏆
JAY: $100 prize 👀 U in Troy?
MIA: Ms. Linn won't notice. She's clueless 😜
TROY: But the quiz…
ZAK: CHILL. We'll cover U. Or U scared? 😒

🚪 **10:55 a.m. — SCHOOL HALLWAY**
Troy's stomach churned. He typed:
"If I say no = 'teacher's pet'… Mom finds out? GROUNDED."
(Sent): k fine

🎮 **11:30 a.m. — ARCADE**
ZAK: POST THIS VID! #SkipSquad 😎
[Video: Troy at game. Ms. Linn's blue hybrid in window.]
JAY: OMG IS THAT HER CAR?? 😳
TROY: DELETE IT NOW!!!

✉ 12:15 p.m. — SCHOOL EMAIL
SUBJECT: UNEXCUSED ABSENCE
Parents notified. Disciplinary action is pending.

GRAMMAR FOCUS — FIXING FRAGMENTS

✗ **Problem:** Fragments = incomplete thoughts. **MISSING PARTS!**

QUICK COMPREHENSION SNAPSHOT

Element	Evidence from Text
Peer-pressure line	"Or are you scared?"
Turning-point image	Ms. Linn's car in the arcade video
Immediate consequence	School email to parents
Internal conflict	Troy's fear of social ridicule vs. parental trust

Diagnostic Chart

Fragment Type	Example Fragment	Revised Complete Sentence
Missing subject	Tagging Troy.	**Zak was** tagging Troy in the post.
Missing verb	After the arcade.	Panic **started** after the arcade.
Dependent clause only	Because he was scared.	He lied **because he was scared**.
-ing opener	Skipping class again.	He **was** skipping class again.
Time phrase	Before lunch.	**We met** before lunch.

Repair Kit:

Ask 3 questions:
1. WHO? → Troy
2. DID WHAT? → panicked
3. COMPLETE THOUGHT? → Troy panicked when he saw the car.

Real Talk— Pressure VS. Power

Consequence Tracker

Choice	Why?	Result (24h)	Result (1 month)
Skip	Fear of ridicule	Fun → Panic	Detention, lost phone
Go to class	Self-respect	FOMO	Trust, quiz credit

Character Motivation Matrix

Character	Action	Underlying Need	Evidence
Zak	Urges skipping	Wants status & thrill	"Skip 4th period… Or are you scared?"
Troy	Follows crowd	Seeks acceptance	Internal monologue reveals fear of ridicule
Jay	Records video	Social media validation	Posts #SkipSquad video
Mia	Minimizes risk	Normalizes defiance	"Ms. Linn won't notice"

Ethical Lens – Discussion Prompts

1. **Integrity vs. Popularity:** Which mattered more to Troy in the moment? Why?
2. **Digital Footprints:** How can a 10-second video reshape a student's record?
3. **Bystander Power:** What could Jay or Mia have done differently?

Role-Play Scenario

Cue: Zak says, "You're no fun anymore."
Task: Craft a one-sentence response that is firm, respectful, and grammatically complete—no fragments allowed.

Chapter Summary

This chapter demonstrates how seemingly minor decisions—nudged by peer-pressure rhetoric—can cascade into significant academic and personal consequences. Students practiced:

- **Reading skills:** parsing digital dialogue and inner narrative to infer motivation.
- **Writing skills:** diagnosing and repairing sentence fragments, a high-frequency exam error.
- **Critical thinking**: mapping cause-and-effect chains and evaluating ethical choices.

Mastering these competencies equips learners to communicate with precision and to navigate social dynamics responsibly—both on campus and online.

📝 Grammar + Story Integration Table: Fix the Fragments in Context

Original Fragment	Why It's Incomplete	Corrected Sentence (Contextual)
After the arcade.	Missing subject and verb	Troy started panicking after the arcade.
Skipping class again.	Lacks a verb	He was skipping class again, just like last week.
Because of peer pressure.	Incomplete thought	He lied because of peer pressure from his friends.
Tagging everyone.	Gerund phrase without subject	Zak was tagging everyone in the arcade video.
Trying to avoid trouble.	Missing subject	Troy was trying to avoid trouble by deleting the post.
Before she noticed.	Dependent clause only	They left the arcade before she noticed the reflection.
Just to impress them.	Incomplete phrase	He skipped class just to impress them.
When he saw the car.	Clause needs a complete sentence	Troy panicked when he saw Ms. Linn's car.
If he had said no.	Dependent clause only	If he had said no, he would've avoided the consequences.
That moment in the hallway.	Sentence lacks action	That moment in the hallway made him question his choice.

ACTIVITY ZONE

ACTIVITY 1 – MULTIPLE-CHOICE STORY RECALL

Mark the best answer.

	Question	a	b	c	d
1	Troy agrees to skip class because	dislikes Ms. Linn	forgot the quiz	wants prize money	fears peer judgment
2	What reveals the truancy?	Arcade staff tip-off	Car in the video	Teacher at arcade	Zak tags school
3	Strongest peer-pressure line?	"Prize = $100"	"We'll cover for you"	"Or are you scared?"	"But the quiz …"
4	Troy's emotion post-video	excitement	panic	relief	confusion
5	First school action	suspension	parent email	counselor referral	detention slip

ACTIVITY 2 – IDENTIFY THE FRAGMENT

Indicate F if Sentence A is a fragment, S if Sentence B is a

Q	Sentence A	Sentence B
1	After the bell rang.	We hurried inside.
2	Skipping class again.	The principal noticed.
3	Because he was nervous.	Troy deleted the post.
4	They posted the video.	When Jay saw the car.
5	Mia cheered.	Tagging everyone.

ACTIVITY 3 – FRAGMENT REPAIR

Rewrite each fragment as a complete, formal sentence.

Fragment	Your Revision
After school ended.	
Trying to impress everyone.	
Skipping again.	
Before the quiz.	
Because he panicked.	

ACTIVITY 4 – CONSEQUENCE REASONING

Respond in one grammatically complete sentence.

Prompt	Response
1. Short-term benefit Troy expected	
2. Long-term academic impact	
3. Respectful refusal line Troy could use	
4. Possible group reaction if Troy declined	
5. Personal value Troy compromised	

ANSWERS
🎯 ACTIVITY ZONE

ACTIVITY 1 – MULTIPLE-CHOICE STORY RECALL

1 d · 2 b · 3 c · 4 b · 5 b

ACTIVITY 2 – IDENTIFY THE FRAGMENT

1 F · 2 F · 3 F · 4 S · 5 S

ACTIVITY 3 – FRAGMENT REPAIR

- We walked home after school ended.
- He was trying to impress everyone.
- He was skipping class again.
- Troy reviewed his notes before the quiz.
- He deleted the post because he panicked.

ACTIVITY 4 – CONSEQUENCE REASONING

- He expected social approval and a chance at prize money.
- Missing the quiz resulted in a zero that lowered his average.
- "I'd rather stay; my grades matter to me."
- They might tease him briefly, then head to the arcade without him.
- He sacrificed honesty for popularity.

Chapter 3 : TEXT ME LATER

One emoji. One comma. One friendship in trouble.)

CHAPTER 3 – TEXT ME LATER

Learning Objectives:

☑ I can recognize how punctuation impacts tone and meaning in dialogue.
☑ I can correctly punctuate speech using commas and quotation marks.
☑ I can infer emotional context and intent from digital messages.
☑ I can match quotes with the correct speakers and interpret dramatic tension.

STORY — TEXT ME LATER

IA story about how shade, screenshots, and a missing comma can wreck a squad.

9:03 p.m. — Group Chat: The Crew

MIA: Yo, Ethan's late AGAIN 😕
JAYDEN: Bro, it's Ethan o'clock fr 😂
ETHAN: Chill, I'm like 2 mins out 🏃‍♂️
MIA: "Sorry, was perfecting my playlist" 😒
JAYDEN: Bet we're still waiting at 10 😑

Private Message — Ethan texts Jayden:

"Wow, real nice, fam. I'm out here rushing 🙃"

Jayden replies:

"Dude, it's a joke. You good?"

10:15 p.m. — Social Media Post

@EthanVibes: "Squad goals: clown you in the group chat 😫 #RealOnesDon't"
Mia comments: "Wait, what?"
Jayden (DM to Mia): "He screenshotted me! Totally twisted my words."

Digital Drama Breakdown

Event	Details
Conflict Trigger	Group chat shade thrown at Ethan
Escalation	Ethan's private text to Jayden
Climax	Ethan posts a screenshot publicly
Aftershock	Trust takes a hit; messages get misread and friends feel hurt

Grammar Focus — Commas in Dialogue

Table: Correct vs. Messy Texts

Incorrect	Correct	Why It Matters
I'm out Ethan said.	"I'm out," Ethan said.	Comma separates dialogue from the speaker tag.
Chill Mia yelled.	"Chill," Mia yelled.	Avoids run-on sentence.
Yo Jayden Ethan snapped.	"Yo, Jayden," Ethan snapped.	Shows who's being addressed.
This is wack Jayden muttered.	"This is wack," Jayden muttered.	Reflects natural rhythm of speech.
Mia said I'm done.	Mia said, "I'm done."	Correct placement of comma and quote marks.

Checklist: Does Your Dialogue Work?

Check This	✅ / ❌
Are quotation marks around spoken words?	
Is there a comma before the dialogue tag?	
Are names in direct address offset by commas?	
Does punctuation reflect the tone?	

💡 Comma Game-Changer:
"Let's chill Ethan." ≠ "Let's chill, Ethan." One comma changes a command into a hangout invite!

Reflection — Tone, Texts & Trusts

Discussion Prompts

- Ever had a text get totally misread? What happened?
- Do emojis make tone clearer or messier?
- Is it ever okay to post a screenshot of a private chat?

Vibe Check Tracker

Action	Why It Went Down	Instant Vibe	Friendship Fallout
Group chat shade	Teasing felt normal	Funny to some, shady to Ethan	Squad feels split
Ethan's private text	Felt attacked, clapped back	Hurt, defensive	Tension spikes
Screenshot post	Wanted to call out the shade	Bold but messy	Trust gets wrecked

Visual Learning Tools

Emoji	Tone It Shows	Example from Story	Impact on the Vibe
🙄	Sarcasm, annoyance	"Yo, Ethan's late AGAIN 🙄"	Makes Ethan feel targeted
😂	Humor, teasing	"Bro, it's Ethan o'clock fr 😂"	Feels fun to Jayden, shady to Ethan
🙃	Hurt, sarcasm	"Wow, real nice, fam. I'm out here rushing 🙃"	Shows Ethan's frustration
😐	Boredom, irritation	"Bet we're still waiting at 10 😐"	Adds to the group's shade
😒	Mocking, annoyed	"Sorry, was perfecting my playlist" 😒	Makes the teasing feel personal

Punctuation Fixes at a Glance — Dialogue Repair Cheatsheet

Problem	Fix It	Example
No quotation marks	Add " " around spoken words	I'm done → "I'm done"
Missing comma	Add comma before tag	I'm done Ethan said → "I'm done," Ethan said
Run-on dialogue	Separate speech and tag	Chill Mia yelled → "Chill," Mia yelled
Name not offset	Add commas around name	Yo Jayden Ethan said → "Yo, Jayden," Ethan said
Wrong quote start	Comma after speaker	Mia said I'm out → Mia said, "I'm out"

Mind Map 1: Digital Drama Flow — What Went Wrong?

Central Idea: Text Me Later Story

- **Conflict**: Group chat shade (😕, 😂) → Ethan feels attacked
- **Escalation**: Ethan's private text (🙄) → Jayden's "it's a joke" reply
- **Climax:** Ethan's screenshot post (@EthanVibes) → Mia's "Wait, what?" comment
- **Fallout:** Trust breaks · Misread vibes · Public drama

Mind Map 2: Punctuation Power — Why Commas Matter

Central Idea: Commas Save Conversations

- **Clarity:** Separates who's talking → "Chill," Mia yelled
- **Tone**: Matches real speech patterns → "Yo, Jayden," Ethan snapped
- **Avoids Confusion**: Prevents run-ons → "I'm out," Ethan said
- **Drama Control:** Right comma = right vibe → "Let's chill, Ethan" vs. "Let's chill Ethan"

Chapter Summary

This chapter dives into how texts, emojis, and punctuation can make or break friendships. A missing comma or shady tone can spark major drama. Teens practiced:

- Nailing dialogue with commas and quotation marks
- Reading tone and intent in messages
- Thinking about ethics around screenshots and digital trust

ACTIVITY ZONE

ACTIVITY 1 – WHO SAID WHAT?

Match the quote to the speaker.

Quote	Who Said It?
"Bet we're still waiting at 10 😒"	
"Wow, real nice, fam. I'm out here rushing 🙄"	
"Yo, Jayden,"	
"Sorry, was perfecting my playlist" ☹	
"Dude, it's a joke. You good?"	

ACTIVITY 2 – FIX THE COMMAS

Add commas and quotation marks to correct each line.
1. I'm over it Mia said
2. Don't clown me Ethan snapped
3. You're wild Jayden laughed
4. Mia said I didn't mean to shade
5. Yo Ethan chill Jayden said

ACTIVITY 3 – REWRITE THE DIALOGUE

Original	Corrected Version
mia said im vibing	
ethan yelled dont post that	
its whatever jayden shrugged	
im not salty mia whispered	
jayden said this is messy	

ACTIVITY 4 – STORY CHECK
(MULTIPLE CHOICE)

1) What set Ethan off?
a) Missing a party
b) Group chat shade he took personally
c) A bad grade
d) Mia's emoji spam

2) Why did Ethan post the screenshot?
a) To flex on the squad
b) He misread the vibe
c) To start a trend
d) To get likes

3) What punctuation could've avoided the drama?
a) A period
b) An exclamation point
c) A comma before the tag
d) A question mark

4) Best way to fix hurt feelings in a chat?
a) Ghost them
b) Post a clapback
c) Talk it out privately
d) Send a meme

5) What's the story's big lesson?
a) Emojis fix everything
b) Tone can get lost in texts
c) Screenshots are always cool
d) Never use group chats

ANSWERS
ACTIVITY ZONE

ACTIVITY 1 – WHO SAID WHAT?

1 = Jayden · 2 = Ethan · 3 = Ethan · 4 = Mia · 5 = Jayden

ACTIVITY 2 – FIX THE COMMAS

1. "I'm over it," Mia said.
2. "Don't clown me," Ethan snapped.
3. "You're wild," Jayden laughed.
4. Mia said, "I didn't mean to shade."
5. "Yo, Ethan, chill," Jayden said.

ACTIVITY 3 – REWRITE THE DIALOGUE

- "I'm vibing," Mia said.
- "Don't post that," Ethan yelled.
- "It's whatever," Jayden shrugged.
- "I'm not salty," Mia whispered.
- Jayden said, "This is messy."

ACTIVITY 4 – STORY CHECK (MULTIPLE CHOICE)

1 = b
2 = b
3 = c
4 = c
5 = b

Chapter 4. Late Again

CHAPTER 3 – LATE AGAIN

Why punctuality isn't just about the clock—it's about trust.

Learning Objectives:

☑ I can describe the consequences of being late using story details.

☑ I can identify and fix run-on sentences.

☑ I can explain how punctuality affects relationships.

☑ I can apply punctuality strategies to real-life scenarios.

STORY — Jamal's Bad Day

Morning Mayhem

Jamal was always running late. His alarm buzzed at 6:30 a.m. He hit snooze. Then he hit it again. By 7:00, he was still in bed. School started at 8:00.

"Jamal, move it!" his mom shouted.

He jumped up. His shirt was wrinkled. His shoes were missing. "Ugh, where's my backpack?" he groaned. He grabbed a granola bar and ran out the door. The bus was gone. Jamal sprinted to school, sweating.

He slid into math class at 8:15.

"Late again, Jamal," Ms. Carter said. "You missed the quiz."

His friends whispered, "Man, you're always late." Jamal felt his face turn red.

Afternoon Trouble

After school, Jamal worked at the pizza shop. His boss, Mr. Lee, was strict.
"Be here at 4:00 sharp," Mr. Lee always said.
Jamal got there at 4:20. A customer was already waiting.
"Jamal, you're late. I can't trust you to open the shop now," Mr. Lee said.
Jamal's stomach sank. He liked his job. He needed the money for new sneakers.
"I'm sorry," he mumbled. "My bus was late."
Mr. Lee shook his head. "You said that last week. You need to plan better."

A Fresh Start

That night, Jamal set two alarms. He laid out his clothes. He packed his bag. The next day, he was on time.
Ms. Carter smiled. "Nice job, Jamal."
Mr. Lee gave him a thumbs-up at work. Jamal grinned. Being on time felt good.

Mind Map: Jamal's Morning Fix

Being Late
- Overslept → Hit snooze → Woke at 7:00
- Disorganized → Clothes missing → Missed bus
- Result → Missed quiz + upset boss
- Solution → Set alarms + prepared clothes → Arrived early

Why It Matters: Jamal's story shows how being late can hurt trust—but small changes can make a big difference.

Grammar Focus— Run-On Sentences

What's a Run-On?

A run-on sentence happens when two complete thoughts are mashed together without punctuation.

Run-On: "Jamal was late; he missed the bus."
Fixed: "Jamal was late. He missed the bus."

How to Fix Run-Ons

1. **Add a Period** — Split into two sentences.
2. **Use a Comma + Conjunction** — Join with words like "and," "but," or "so."
3. **Use a Semicolon** — Join two related sentences with a semicolon (;).

Table: Break the Sentence

Run-On Sentence	Fixed Sentence	Fix Used
Jamal woke up late he ran to school.	Jamal woke up late. He ran to school.	Period
He missed the bus he was late for class.	He missed the bus, so he was late for class.	Comma + "so"
His boss was mad he didn't trust Jamal.	His boss was mad; he didn't trust Jamal.	Semicolon
Jamal set two alarms he got to work early.	Jamal set two alarms, and he got to work early.	Comma + "and"
School started at 8:00 Jamal got there late.	School started at 8:00. Jamal got there late.	Period

Run-On Radar: Grammar Tip Box

If you find more than one subject and verb in a sentence with no punctuation— It's likely a run-on!

Flowchart: How to Fix a Run-On

Is it a Run-On?
- Yes → Two complete thoughts?
  - Add a Period → "I was late. I ran."
  - Add Comma + Conjunction → "I was late, so I ran."
  - Add Semicolon → "I was late; I ran."
- No → Sentence is fine

Real Talk — Why Punctuality Matters

Discussion Prompts

- What does being on time say about you?
- Why did Jamal's teacher and boss react the way they did?
- What's one morning habit you could change?

Table: Being On Time vs. Being Late

Being On Time	Being Late
Teachers trust you	Teachers get upset
Boss gives you more tasks	Boss takes away duties
Friends respect you	Friends feel ignored
You feel proud	You feel stressed

Quick Write

Write about a time you were late. How did it affect others? What would you change next time?

ACTIVITY ZONE

ACTIVITY 1 – STORY COMPREHENSION (TRUE/FALSE)

1. Jamal was always on time for school.
2. Jamal's boss was happy when he was late
3. Jamal set two alarms to be on time.
4. Ms. Carter smiled when Jamal was late.
5. Jamal wanted new sneakers.

ACTIVITY 2 – FIX THE RUN-ON

Which option correctly fixes: "I was late I forgot my bag."

1. a) I was late. I forgot my bag.
2. b) I was late, so I forgot my bag.
3. c) I was late; I forgot my bag.
4. d) I was late I forgot my bag.
5. e) I was late I forgot, my bag.

ACTIVITY 3 – PUNCTUALITY CHOICES

What should you do to be on time? Choose the best answer for each situation.

1. School starts at 8:00 → Wake up at...
2. Work starts at 4:00 → Leave at...
3. Bus at 7:30 → Arrive by...
4. Test at 9:00 → Study...
5. Party at 6:00 → Arrive at...

ACTIVITY 4 – REAL TALK REFLECTION

Answer these questions about being on time. Choose the best answer for each.

1. Being on time shows…
2. Teachers get upset because…
3. One way to be on time…
4. Being late makes you feel…
5. Why did Mr. Lee lose trust?

ACTIVITY 5 – REAL-LIFE PROBLEM SOLVING

Read each situation and choose the best solution.

1. Jamal's bus was late again. What should he do tomorrow?
2. You forgot to set your alarm. What can you do to avoid this?
3. You keep losing your homework in the morning. How can you fix it?
4. You arrive late to class three times this week. What should you reflect on?
5. Your teacher says, "You're always rushing in." What's one change you could try?

ANSWERS
🎯 ACTIVITY ZONE

ACTIVITY 1 – STORY COMPREHENSION (TRUE/FALSE)

1. Jamal was always on time for school. → False
2. Jamal's boss was happy when he was late. → False
3. Jamal set two alarms to be on time. → True
4. Ms. Carter smiled when Jamal was late. → False
5. Jamal wanted new sneakers. → True

ACTIVITY 2 – FIX THE RUN-ON

- a) I was late. I forgot my bag. ☑ Fix the Run-On

ACTIVITY 3 – PUNCTUALITY CHOICES

- School starts at 8:00 → Wake up at… c) 6:30
- Work starts at 4:00 → Leave at… b) 3:30
- Bus at 7:30 → Arrive by… a) 7:25
- Test at 9:00 → Study… b) Night before
- Party at 6:00 → Arrive at… a) 5:50

ACTIVITY 4 – REAL TALK REFLECTION

- Being on time shows… a) You're reliable
- Teachers get upset because… a) You miss learning
- One way to be on time… a) Set an alarm
- Being late makes you feel… b) Stressed
- Why did Mr. Lee lose trust? a) Jamal was late
- What did Jamal do differently to improve his punctuality? a) He set alarms and prepared ahead

ACTIVITY 5 – REAL-LIFE PROBLEM SOLVING

- Set an earlier backup alarm
- Set a repeating alarm on a phone or clock
- Pack your bag the night before
- Your morning routine and time spent getting ready
- Prepare earlier and leave home with buffer time

Chapter 5. NO FILTER

CHAPTER 5 – NO FILTER

How one post can go too far — and what to do when it does.

Learning Objectives:

☑ I can describe how online posts can impact relationships.

☑ I can use "your" and "you're" correctly in captions and writing.

☑ I can reflect on responsible social media use.

☑ I can edit and improve posts before sharing.

STORY — Maya's Mistake

Viral Gone Wrong

Maya loved TikTok. She posted dance videos daily. Her friends loved them. She had 500 followers.

"I'm gonna go viral!" she told her best friend, Liam.

One day, Maya was upset. Liam borrowed her favorite hoodie and spilled soda on it.

"Ugh, Liam, you're so clumsy!" she snapped.

Liam chuckled. "Sorry, Maya. I'll wash it."

But Maya stayed mad. At lunch, she recorded Liam tripping in the hallway. She added text: "My friend ruins everything." She posted it without thinking.

By dinner, it had 10,000 views. Likes poured in.

Liam texted: "Why'd you post that? Everyone's laughing at me."

Maya's heart dropped. "It was just a joke," she replied.

Liam didn't respond. At school, kids whispered.

"There's the clumsy guy!"

Liam looked down. At lunch, he sat alone. Maya felt awful. Her post hurt her best friend.

She deleted the video. Then posted: "Liam's my best friend. I messed up. I'm sorry."

"I was dumb," she said in person. "Can we be friends again?"

Liam nodded. "Just think before you post, okay?"

Maya smiled—no more posts without a filter.

Mind Map: Maya's Post Impact

Maya's Post
- Action: Posts Liam tripping w/ caption
- Result: Video goes viral → 10,000 views
- Problem: Liam hurt, friendship breaks
- Solution: Deletes post → Public apology → Talks to Liam

Why This Matters: Maya learned that one joke online can hurt someone offline. A smart post protects both your rep and your relationships.

Grammar Focus — Homophones: Your vs. You're

What Are Homophones?

Homophones are words that sound the same but have different meanings and spellings. Example:

- **Your** = something that belongs to you ("Your phone is on the table.")
- **You're** = short for "you are" ("You're awesome!")

How to Choose the Right One

If you mean...	Use	Example
Something that belongs to you	**your**	"Your dance moves are cool."
You are doing something	**you're**	"You're going viral!"

Table: Homophone Fixes in Social Media Captions

Incorrect Caption	Correct Caption	Why?
Your so clumsy, Liam!	You're so clumsy, Liam!	"You're" = You are
I love you're dance moves!	I love your dance moves!	"Your" = Dance moves belong to you
Your going viral!	You're going viral!	"You're" = You are going viral
Is this you're phone?	Is this your phone?	"Your" = Phone belongs to someone
Your my best friend.	You're my best friend.	"You're" = You are my best friend

Tip Box: Quick Homophone Check

Try saying "you are" instead. If it works, use "you're." If not, use "your."

Real Talk — Think Before You Post

Discussion Prompts

- Can you undo a post once it's live?
- Why do captions and emojis matter?
- What happens when humor goes too far?
- When should you ask permission before posting?

Table: Posting With Care vs. Without

Without Thinking	With Thinking
Hurts feelings	Builds trust
Goes viral for wrong reason	Goes viral for something kind
Gets screenshotted forever	Shows maturity
Embarrasses others	Celebrates others

🎯 ACTIVITY ZONE

ACTIVITY 1 – STORY COMPREHENSION

1. What video did Maya post?
2. How did Liam feel after seeing the post?
3. How many views did the video get?
4. What did Maya do after she saw Liam upset?
5. What did Maya post next?

ACTIVITY 2 – HOMOPHONE FIXES

1. Your my best friend.
2. You're phone is ringing.
3. I love your new haircut!
4. Your going to regret that!
5. You're the nicest person I know.

ACTIVITY 3 – SOCIAL MEDIA SCENARIOS

1. You record a silly video of a friend. What do you do before posting?
2. You're angry after a fight. What's a safer move than posting?
3. Your post might seem mean. What should you do?
4. You see a post shaming someone. What should you do?
5. You want a post to go viral. What type of post is best?

ACTIVITY 4 – REAL TALK REFLECTION

1. Why do captions matter?
2. Why did Maya regret posting the video?
3. What could she have done before posting?
4. What did Liam say at the end?
5. What's one rule you'll use when posting now?

ACTIVITY 5 – EDITING CHALLENGE

Rewrite the incorrect captions using the correct homophone.

1. Your late again!
2. You're dance video is cool.
3. Is this you're backpack?
4. Your amazing at basketball!
5. You're homework is on the desk.

ACTIVITY 6 – CAPTION CREATOR

Create the most respectful and correct version of each social media post. Fix grammar, replace poor word choices, and think before you post! Use the proper form of your or you're.

Instructions: Rewrite each caption so it's clear, kind, and grammatically correct.

1. your such a loser lol 😂
2. you're dog is ugly 🐶💀
3. Can't believe your that clumsy...
4. you're just jealous of me 😒
5. Your so annoying, don't text me ...

48

ANSWERS
🎯 ACTIVITY ZONE

ACTIVITY 1 – STORY COMPREHENSION

1. A video of Liam tripping with a mean caption.
2. He felt embarrassed and hurt.
3. 10,000 views.
4. She deleted the video and apologized.
5. A public apology post.

ACTIVITY 2 – HOMOPHONE FIXES

1. You're my best friend.
2. Your phone is ringing.
3. Correct as is.
4. You're going to regret that!
5. Correct as is.

ACTIVITY 3 – SOCIAL MEDIA SCENARIOS

1. Ask for permission.
2. Talk to someone offline or write it down.
3. Pause, reread, and don't post.
4. Tell a trusted adult or report it.
5. Something kind, creative, or inspiring.

ACTIVITY 4 – REAL TALK REFLECTION

1. Set an earlier backup alarm
2. Set a repeating alarm on a phone or clock
3. Pack your bag the night before
4. Your morning routine and time spent getting ready
5. Prepare earlier and leave home with buffer time

ACTIVITY 5 – EDITING CHALLENGE

1. You're late again!
2. Your dance video is cool.
3. Is this your backpack?
4. You're amazing at basketball!
5. Your homework is on the desk.

ACTIVITY 6 – CAPTION CREATOR

1. You're such a good sport! 😄 (Positive twist + correct homophone)
2. Your dog is cute in their own way. 🐶 (Empathetic + correct word)
3. You're not usually that clumsy. Are you okay? (Supportive tone + correct usage)
4. You're amazing, no need to compare! (Encouraging + correct grammar)
5. You're bugging me right now. Let's talk later. 😶 (Respectful and honest)

Chapter 6. THE GROUP PROJECT

CHAPTER 6 – THE GROUP PROJECT

What happens when one person does all the work — and how to fix it.

Learning Objectives:

☑ I can explain why fairness matters in group projects.

☑ I can identify and fix subject-verb agreement errors.

☑ I can describe how to advocate when teamwork feels unfair.

☑ I can build stronger group plans for shared success.

STORY —Ava's Heavy Load

The Solo Struggle

Ava was excited about the science project. Her group had to make a poster about planets. The teacher, Mr. Diaz, said, "Everyone must help. It's due Friday." Ava's group had four kids: Ava, Sam, Lila, and Jay.

Ava loved science. She made a plan. "I'll research Mars," she said. "Sam, you do Jupiter. Lila, do Venus. Jay, make the poster." Everyone nodded. Ava thought it would be easy.

But Sam didn't do his part. He played games on his phone. Lila said, "I'm too busy." Jay forgot to buy poster board. By Wednesday, Ava was worried. The project was due in two days!

Ava stayed up late. She researched all the planets. She drew the poster. Her hands hurt from writing. On Friday, she brought the poster to class. It looked great. Mr. Diaz said, "Nice work, team!" Sam, Lila, and Jay smiled like they helped.

Ava was mad. She did everything! At lunch, she told her group, "I did all the work. That's not fair." Sam shrugged. "Chill, we got an A." Lila said, "You're good at science." Jay just looked away.

Ava took a deep breath. "We need to talk to Mr. Diaz," she said. They went to the teacher. Ava explained, "I did the whole project." Mr. Diaz frowned. "Teamwork means everyone helps. You three need to do better next time."

Sam, Lila, and Jay apologized. They promised to help on the next project. Ava felt proud. Speaking up was hard, but it worked.

Mind Map: Ava's Group Project

```
Group Project
    ├──── Plan: Everyone gets a job
    │      ├──── Ava: Research Mars
    │      ├──── Sam: Research Jupiter
    │      ├──── Lila: Research Venus
    │      └──── Jay: Make poster
    ├──── Problem: Ava does everything
    │      ├──── Sam plays games
    │      ├──── Lila is busy
    │      └──── Jay forgets poster
    ├──── Result: Ava's upset
    │      ├──── Works alone
    │      └──── Group takes credit
    └──── Solution: Speaks up
           ├──── Talks to group
           ├──── Tells teacher
           └──── Group apologizes
```

Why This Matters: Ava's story shows that silence in group work can feel unfair, and speaking up can create change.

Grammar Focus — Subject-Verb Agreement

What Is Subject-Verb Agreement?

The subject and the verb in a sentence must match. Singular subjects need singular verbs. Plural subjects need plural verbs.

- Singular: Ava works hard.
- Plural: Ava and Sam work hard.

Tips for Agreement

Subject Type	Use...	Example
Singular (he, Ava)	Verb + "s"	Ava **works** on the poster.
Plural (they, Sam & Lila)	Verb without "s"	Sam and Lila **help** out.
Tricky (everyone)	Treat as singular	Everyone **brings** supplies.

Table: Make It Agree!

Incorrect Sentence	Correct Sentence	Why?
Ava work too much.	Ava **works** too much.	"Ava" is singular, so use "works."
The group forget the poster.	The group **forgets** the poster.	"Group" is singular. Add "s" to verb.
Sam and Lila plays games.	Sam and Lila **play** games.	Plural subject → verb without "s"
Everyone help on the project.	Everyone **helps** on the project.	"Everyone" is treated as singular.
The teams does well.	The teams **do** well.	"Teams" is plural → use "do."

Flowchart: Does Your Subject and Verb Agree?

Check the Subject
- Is it singular? (he, she, it, Ava, group)
  - Yes: Use verb with "s" → e.g., "Ava works."
  - No → Check if it's plural (they, teams)
    - Use verb without "s" → "They work."
- Is it a tricky subject? (everyone, nobody)
  - Treat as singular → "Everyone helps."

Real Talk — Sharing The Load

Discussion Prompts

- What makes a group project fair?
- Have you ever had to do more work than others? How did it feel?
- Why do some people stay silent in unfair groups?
- What can you do to make sure everyone helps?

Table: Fair vs. Unfair Group Work

Fair Group Work	Unfair Group Work
Everyone has a clear role	One person does everything
Group checks in regularly	No one communicates
Credit is shared fairly	Group takes credit unfairly
Team speaks up respectfully	Issues are ignored

ACTIVITY ZONE

ACTIVITY 1 - STORY COMPREHENSION

1) Ava did all the work on the project.
a) True
b) False
c) Sometimes
d) Never
e) Not in the story

2) Sam helped with the poster.
a) True
b) False
c) Sometimes
d) Always
e) Not in the story

3) Ava told Mr. Diaz about the group.
 1. a) True
 2. b) False
 3. c) Sometimes
 4. d) Never
 5. e) Not in the story

4) The project was about animals.
a) True
b) False
c) Sometimes
d) Always
e) Not in the story

5) The group apologized to Ava.
a) True
b) False
c) Sometimes
d) Never
e) Not in the story

ACTIVITY 2 –GRAMMAR CHECK — SUBJECT-VERB FIXES

1) The team work hard.
a) Correct
b) Incorrect
c) Needs "works"
d) Needs a comma
e) Needs a period

2) Ava and Sam helps out.
a) Correct
b) Incorrect
c) Needs "help"
d) Needs a semicolon
e) Needs a conjunction

3) Everyone does their part.
a) Correct
b) Incorrect
c) Needs "do"
d) Needs a comma
e) Needs a period

4) The group makes a plan.
a) Correct
b) Incorrect
c) Needs "make"
d) Needs a semicolon
e) Needs a conjunction

5) Lila forget her task.
1. a) Correct
2. b) Incorrect
3. c) Needs "forgets"
4. d) Needs a comma
5. e) Needs a period

ACTIVITY 3 – GROUP PROJECT SCENARIOS

1) Your group has a project due.
a) Do all the work
b) Make a plan together
c) Skip meetings
d) Let one person lead
e) Forget the deadline

2) Someone isn't helping.
a) Ignore it
b) Talk to them
c) Do their work
d) Tell everyone else
e) Give up

3) The project is due tomorrow.
a) Stay up all night
b) Check in with the group
c) Skip it
d) Blame someone
e) Copy another group

4) You're good at drawing.
a) Do all the art
b) Teach others to help
c) Don't do anything
d) Hide your skills
e) Take over the project

5) The teacher asks who did what.
a) Lie about it
b) Tell the truth
c) Say nothing
d) Blame the group
e) Laugh it off

ACTIVITY 4 – REAL TALK REFLECTION

1) What makes a group project fair?
a) One person does all
b) Everyone helps
c) No one plans
d) You skip it
e) You fight

2) Why did Ava feel mad?
a) She got an A
b) She did all the work
c) The group helped
d) The project was easy
e) She liked science

3) How can you make sure everyone helps?
a) Do it alone
b) Make a plan
c) Ignore the group
d) Miss meetings
e) Blame others

4) How does unfair group work feel?
a) Fun
b) Stressful
c) Exciting
d) Easy
e) Happy

5) Why did Ava talk to Mr. Diaz?

a) To get an A
b) To tell the truth
c) To skip the project
d) To blame Sam
e) To quit the group

ANSWERS
ACTIVITY ZONE

ACTIVITY 1 – STORY COMPREHENSION

1. a) True
2. b) False
3. a) True
4. b) False
5. a) True

ACTIVITY 2 – GRAMMAR CHECK

1. c) Needs "works"
2. c) Needs "help"
3. a) Correct
4. a) Correct
5. c) Needs "forgets"

ACTIVITY 3 – GROUP PROJECT SCENARIOS

1. b) Make a plan together
2. b) Talk to them
3. b) Check in with the group
4. b) Teach others to help
5. b) Tell the truth

ACTIVITY 4 – REAL TALK REFLECTION

1. b) Everyone helps
2. b) She did all the work
3. b) Make a plan
4. b) Stressful
5. b) To tell the truth

Chapter 7. FAKE IT 'TIL YOU BREAK IT

CHAPTER 7 – FAKE IT TIL YOU BREAK IT

What happens when online lies get real?

Learning Objectives:

☑ I can explain how fake posts can hurt relationships.

☑ I can choose the correct pronoun in a sentence.

☑ I can recognize the value of being honest online.

☑ I can revise posts to reflect my true identity

STORY —The Fake Profile Fiasco

Eli's Big Lie

Eli was shy. At school, he didn't talk much. But online, he could be anyone. On Instagram, he made a fake profile. He called himself "CoolEli23." He posted pictures of fancy cars and beaches. He said he was a DJ. Kids at school followed him. They thought he was cool.

Eli's classmate, Tara, messaged him. "Wow, you're a DJ? That's awesome!" Eli felt great. He kept lying. "Yeah, I play big shows," he wrote. Tara invited him to the school talent show. "Show us your DJ skills!" she said.

Eli panicked. He wasn't a DJ. He didn't even own a speaker. At school, kids asked about "CoolEli23." "Is that you?" Tara asked. Eli's face got red. "Uh, no," he mumbled. But Tara saw his phone. It had the "CoolEli23" account open.

"You lied!" Tara said. Kids whispered. Eli felt small. His fake profile made him popular, but now everyone laughed. Tara was mad. "Why'd you pretend?" she asked. Eli shrugged. "I wanted to be cool.

Eli deleted "CoolEli23." He messaged Tara. "I'm sorry. I'm just Eli. I like video games, not DJing."

Tara replied, "Just be you. That's cool enough." Eli smiled. He learned to be real.

Mind Map: Eli's Fake Profile Journey

```
Eli's Fake Profile
├── Creates "CoolEli23"
│   ├── Posts fake pics
│   └── Pretends to be DJ
├── Gets Popular
│   ├── Kids follow him
│   └── Tara reaches out
├── Trouble Hits
│   ├── Truth is exposed
│   └── Friends feel betrayed
└── Makes It Right
    ├── Deletes account
    ├── Apologizes
    └── Shows true self
```

Grammar Focus — Pronoun Power : He, She, They

What Are Pronouns?

Pronouns take the place of nouns in writing. They make sentences smoother and help avoid repetition.

Common Pronouns

Type	Examples	Usage
Subject	he, she, they	"He went home."
Object	him, her, them	"I saw her at school."
Possessive	his, her, their	"That is his phone."

Table: Pronoun Corrections from the Story

Incorrect Sentence	Correct Sentence	Explanation
Eli made a profile. She lied.	Eli made a profile. He lied.	"Eli" is a boy → use "he."
Tara was mad. He yelled at Eli.	Tara was mad. She yelled at Eli.	"Tara" is a girl → use "she."
The kids laughed. He saw the phone.	The kids laughed. They saw it.	"Kids" is plural → use "they."
Eli lost her followers.	Eli lost his followers.	"Eli" is male → use "his."
Eli and Tara talked. He made up.	Eli and Tara talked. They made up.	"Eli and Tara" is plural → use "they."

Flowchart: Choose the Right Pronoun

Choosing a Pronoun
├── One person?
│   ├── Boy → he/his
│   ├── Girl → she/her
│   └── Unknown/Nonbinary → they/their
└── More than one person?
    └── Use they/their

Real Talk — Being Real Online

Being honest online can be hard. It's tempting to seem cooler or more popular. But real friendships are built on truth. Eli learned that the hard way.

Discussion Questions

- Why do people pretend online?
- What happens when your lie is exposed?
- How does being honest build trust?
- Have you ever seen a fake post online?
- How can you support someone being real?

Table: Real vs. Fake Online Behavior

Being Fake Online	Being Real Online
Gets fast likes	Builds true connections
May hurt others	Shows respect
Creates stress	Brings peace of mind
Based on lies	Based on honesty

Real-Life Connection: Think of someone who always posts the truth, even if it's not flashy. What makes you respect them?

ACTIVITY ZONE

ACTIVITY 1 – STORY COMPREHENSION

1) **Eli made a fake Instagram profile.**

a) True
b) False
c) Sometimes
d) Never
e) Not in the story

2) **Tara knew Eli was a DJ.**

a) True
b) False
c) Sometimes
d) Always
e) Not in the story

3) **Eli apologized to Tara.**

a) True
b) False
c) Sometimes
d) Never
e) Not in the story

4) **Eli's fake profile was called "DJStar."**

a) True
b) False
c) Sometimes
d) Always
e) Not in the story

5) **Tara forgave Eli.**

a) True
b) False
c) Sometimes
d) Never
e) Not in the story

ACTIVITY 2 – PRONOUN FIXES

1) Eli lied. She felt bad.
a) Correct
b) Incorrect
c) Needs "he"
d) Needs a comma
e) Needs a period

2) Tara was mad. They yelled at Eli.
a) Correct
b) Incorrect
c) Needs "she"
d) Needs a semicolon
e) Needs a conjunction

3) The kids followed Eli. They liked his posts.
a) Correct
b) Incorrect
c) Needs "he"
d) Needs a comma
e) Needs a period

4) Eli lost her followers.

a) Correct
b) Incorrect
c) Needs "his"
d) Needs a semicolon
e) Needs a conjunction

5) Eli and Tara talked. He made up.

a) Correct
b) Incorrect
c) Needs "they"
d) Needs a comma
e) Needs a period

ACTIVITY 3 – ONLINE HONESTY SCENARIOS

1) You want to seem cool online.
a) Post fake pictures
b) Share your real hobbies
c) Pretend to be famous
d) Lie about your age
e) Copy someone else

2) Someone asks about your profile.
a) Lie about it
b) Tell the truth
c) Ignore them
d) Make up a story
e) Block them

3) You post something untrue.
a) Keep it up
b) Delete and apologize
c) Add more lies
d) Get more likes
e) Laugh it off

4) Your friend posts a fake story.
a) Like it
b) Talk to them
c) Share it
d) Comment something mean
e) Ignore it

5) The teacher asks who did what.
a) Lie about it
b) Tell the truth
c) Say nothing
d) Blame the group
e) Laugh it off

ACTIVITY 4 – REAL TALK REFLECTION

1) What happens when you fake it online?

a) You make true friends
b) You lose trust
c) You get famous
d) You feel great
e) Nothing happens

2) Why did Eli pretend to be a DJ?

a) He was a real DJ
b) He wanted to be cool
c) He liked music
d) He was bored
e) He hated school

3) How can you be real online?
a) Post fake stories
b) Share true things
c) Lie about your age
d) Pretend to be famous
e) Copy others

4) How did Eli feel when his lie was exposed?
a) Happy
b) Proud
c) Small
d) Excited
e) Calm

5) Why was Tara mad at Eli?
a) He was a DJ
b) He lied online
c) He ignored her
d) He got famous
e) He moved away

We'd Love Your Feedback!

Please let us know how we're doing by leaving us a review.

ANSWERS
ACTIVITY ZONE

ACTIVITY 1 – STORY COMPREHENSION

1.1) a, 2) b, 3) a, 4) b, 5) a

ACTIVITY 2 – PRONOUN FIXES

1) c, 2) c, 3) a, 4) c, 5) c

ACTIVITY 3 – ONLINE HONESTY SCENARIOS

1) b, 2) b, 3) b, 4) b, 5) b

ACTIVITY 4 – REAL TALK REFLECTION

1.1) b, 2) b, 3) b, 4) c, 5) b

Chapter 8. LOCKER ROOM TALK

CHAPTER 8 – LOCKER ROOM TALK

What happens when gossip spreads like wildfire?

Learning Objectives:

☑ I can explain how gossip affects friendships.

☑ I can use quotation marks correctly in direct and indirect speech.

☑ I can reflect on ways to stop rumors and rebuild trust.

☑ I can apply dialogue punctuation in narrative writing.

STORY —The Gossip Trap

Kyla's Big Mistake

Kyla and Mia were tight. They shared secrets after gym class in the locker room. One day, Kyla was upset. Mia had made the soccer team—but Kyla hadn't. "Mia's not even good," Kyla told Sarah, rolling her eyes. "Her dad's the coach. That's why she got picked."

Sarah gasped. "For real?"

Kyla nodded, though she knew it wasn't true. She was just jealous.
By lunch, whispers buzzed through the cafeteria. "Mia's dad got her on the team," kids said. Mia overheard. Her eyes glistened.

"Kyla, did you say that?" Mia asked.

Kyla's heart dropped. "I didn't mean it," she said quietly. But Mia walked away. She stopped texting Kyla. She sat with new friends. Kyla felt hollow. Gossip had burned her best friend.

After school, Kyla found Mia by the lockers.

"I'm so sorry," Kyla said. "I was jealous. You worked hard and deserved it." Mia frowned. "That really hurt, Kyla. Everyone believed it."

Kyla nodded. "I want to make it right."

She faced the soccer team the next day. "I lied about Mia. She earned her spot. I was wrong."

The team listened. Mia gave a small smile. "Thanks for owning up," she said. Gossip traps you, but honesty sets you free.

Mind Map: Kyla's Gossip Trail

```
Gossip Trouble
├── Starts Rumor
│   ├── Lies about Mia
│   └── Tells Sarah in locker room
├── Rumor Spreads
│   ├── Cafeteria gossip
│   └── Mia overhears
├── Fallout
│   ├── Friendship broken
│   └── Kyla feels guilty
└── Redemption
    ├── Apologizes to Mia
    ├── Tells the team the truth
    └── Rebuilds trust
```

Why This Story Matters: Gossip starts with jealousy, but it can end in regret. Kyla's story teaches how honesty can heal damage.

Grammar Focus — Mastering Quotation Marks

What Are Quotation Marks?

Quotation marks (" ") show someone's exact words. If you're not quoting directly, you use indirect speech.

Form	Example	Rule
Direct Speech	Kyla said, "I was jealous."	Use quotes for exact words
Indirect Speech	Kyla said she was jealous.	No quotes, just summarize the message

Punctuation Rules

- Use commas to introduce quotes: Mia asked, "Did you say that?"
- Keep punctuation inside quotation marks.
- Don't use quotation marks for indirect speech.

Table: Quote It or Sum It Up!

Direct Speech	Indirect Speech	Explanation
Kyla said, "Mia's not even good."	Kyla said Mia wasn't good.	Quote vs. summary
Sarah asked, "For real?"	Sarah asked if it was true.	Question paraphrased
Mia said, "Did you say that?"	Mia asked if Kyla said it.	Changes from exact to indirect speech
Kyla said, "I'm sorry."	Kyla said she was sorry.	No quotes when summarizing
Mia said, "Thanks for owning up."	Mia thanked Kyla for owning up.	Changes to third-person explanation

Flowchart: Should I Use Quotation Marks?

Are you quoting exact words?
- Yes → Use quotation marks
- No → Use indirect speech (no quotes)

Real Talk — Breaking The Rumor Cycle

Rumors can tear apart friendships. They hurt feelings and twist the truth. But one person can stop the cycle.

Discussion Questions
- Why do people spread gossip?
- How did jealousy play a role in Kyla's mistake?
- What did Kyla do to fix things?
- What can you do if you hear a rumor?
- How can schools stop gossip?

Table: Gossip vs. Honesty

Gossip Spreads	Honesty Heals
Hurts people's feelings	Builds trust
Spreads false information	Tells the truth
Destroys friendships	Repairs relationships
Feels easy in the moment	Takes courage but brings peace

Real-Life Connection: Have you ever seen a rumor cause harm? What would you do differently now?

ACTIVITY ZONE

ACTIVITY 1 – QUOTE IT RIGHT!

Match the direct speech with its indirect version.

1. Kyla said, "Mia's not even good."
2. Sarah asked, "For real?"
3. Mia said, "Did you say that?"
4. Kyla said, "I'm so sorry."
5. Mia said, "Thanks for owning up."

A. Kyla said she was sorry.
B. Kyla said Mia wasn't good.
C. Mia asked if Kyla said that.
D. Sarah asked if it was true.
E. Mia thanked Kyla for owning up.

ACTIVITY 2 – FILL-IN-THE-BLANK: FIX THE SENTENCE!

1. Mia said ____ "Did you say that?"
2. Kyla said "I lied." (Needs a ____)
3. Sarah asked For real? (Needs ____)
4. Kyla said ____ was jealous. (Needs pronoun)
5. Mia thanked Kyla for owning up. (Correct as is? Yes/No: ____)

ACTIVITY 3 – RUMOR RESPONSE PICKER

Pick the best action:
1) You hear a rumor about a friend.
a) Spread it b) Ask your friend c) Post it d) Ignore it e) Laugh about it

2) Someone spreads a rumor about you.
a) Fight b) Spread one back c) Tell the truth d) Stay quiet e) Block everyone

3) You shared a rumor accidentally.
a) Hide it b) Apologize c) Laugh d) Share more e) Blame someone else

4) A rumor is hurting a friend.
a) Tell a teacher b) Ignore it c) Repost it d) Joke about it e) Ask others to share it

5) You want to stop gossip.
a) Be kind b) Stay silent c) Start new gossip d) Post drama e) Quit social media

ACTIVITY 4 –REFLECTION QUIZ

1) Why do rumors sting?
a) They build trust b) They hurt feelings c) They're funny d) They go away fast e) They make friends

2) Why did Kyla spread the rumor?
a) She was jealous. b) She was bored. c) She wanted to be popular. d) She was confused. e) She was happy for Mia

3) What helped fix the friendship?
a) A text b) A rumor c) An apology d) Silence e) Ignoring it

4) What do quotation marks show?
   1. a) Feelings b) Speech c) Rumors d) Thoughts e) Anger

5) What did Kyla do at the end?
a) Blamed others b) Lied again c) Told the truth d) Quit the team e) Ignored Mia

ANSWERS
ACTIVITY ZONE

ACTIVITY 1 – MATCHING

1-B, 2-D, 3-C, 4-A, 5-E

ACTIVITY 2 – FILL-IN-THE-BLANK:

1. Mia said, "Did you say that?" — needs a comma before the quote.
2. Kyla said, "I lied." — add a comma before the quote.
3. Sarah asked, "For real?" — needs quotation marks around the quote.
4. Kyla said she was jealous — use the pronoun "she" in indirect speech.
5. Yes — the sentence is already correct.

ACTIVITY 3 – RUMOR PICKER

1-b, 2-c, 3-b, 4-a, 5-a

ACTIVITY 4 – REFLECTION

1-b, 2-a, 3-c, 4-b, 5-c

Chapter 9 : SECOND CHANCE

CHAPTER 9 – SECOND CHANCE

What happens when you mess up and want to make it right?

Learning Objectives:

☑ I can explain why honesty is important, especially after making a mistake.

☑ I can use past and present verb tenses accurately in my writing.

☑ I can reflect on how to respond when tempted to cheat.

☑ I can apply tense rules to make my writing clearer.

STORY — The Cheating Fix

Rico's Big Choice

Rico hated math tests. Numbers made his head spin. His teacher, Ms. Lopez, gave a big test on Friday. "Study hard," she said. "This counts for your grade." Rico didn't study. He was too busy playing video games.

On test day, Rico panicked. He saw his friend Ana's paper. Her answers looked right. Rico copied them. He turned in his test and felt okay. But Ms. Lopez noticed. Both papers had the same wrong answer for question 10. She called Rico and Ana after class.

"Rico, did you copy?" Ms. Lopez asked. Rico's heart raced. He wanted to lie. "No," he started, but his voice shook. Ana looked upset. "I didn't let him copy," she said. Rico felt awful. Ana could get in trouble, too. "I copied," Rico admitted. "Ana didn't know. It's my fault." Ms. Lopez nodded. "Thank you for being honest, Rico.

You get a zero, but you can retake the test next week. Study this time." Ana sighed with relief. "Thanks, Rico," she said.

Rico studied all week. He asked Ana for help. On the retake, he got a C. It wasn't great, but he earned it. Ms. Lopez smiled. "Good job, Rico. Honesty got you a second chance." Rico grinned. Being real felt better than cheating.

Mind Map: Rico's Cheating Trail

```
Cheating Trouble
├── Starts Mistake
│   ├── Doesn't study
│   └── Copies Ana's answers
├── Consequence
│   ├── Ms. Lopez finds out
│   └── Ana almost gets in trouble
├── Turning Point
│   ├── Rico admits it
│   └── Takes the blame
└── Redemption
    ├── Studies with Ana
    ├── Retakes the test
    └── Learns from mistakes
```

Why This Story Matters: Mistakes happen. What matters most is what we do next. Rico's story shows how honesty and effort can help rebuild trust.

Grammar Focus — Get Verb Tenses Right

What Are Verb Tenses?

Verb tenses tell when something happens:
- Past Tense: Already happened → "Rico studied."
- Present Tense: Happening now → "Rico studies."

How to Choose

- Look for time clues like yesterday (past) or now (present).
- Match your verb to the time it happened.

80

Table: "Was vs. Is: Pick the Right Time!"

Incorrect Sentence	Correct Sentence	Explanation
Rico study yesterday.	Rico studied yesterday.	"Yesterday" = past → use past tense.
Ana is upset last week.	Ana was upset last week.	"Last week" = past → use "was."
Ms. Lopez talk now.	Ms. Lopez talks now.	"Now" = present → use present tense.
Rico cheat today.	Rico cheats today.	"Today" = present → use present tense.
They studies last night.	They studied last night.	"Last night" = past → use past tense.

Practice Example

Incorrect: Rico study for the test now.
Correct: Rico studies for the test now.

Why: "Now" means it's happening → use present tense.

Flowchart: Verb Tense Clues

When did it happen?
├── Now → Present tense → Example: "Rico studies."
└── Earlier → Past tense → Example: "Rico studied."

REAL TALK — CHOOSING HONESTY

Cheating may seem like a quick fix, but it can create bigger problems. Rico's story shows how honesty helps repair damage. Let's explore how to choose honesty—even when it's hard.

Discussion Questions

- *Why is cheating unfair to others?*
- *What caused Rico to cheat?*
- *How did his choice affect Ana?*
- *What helped Rico fix his mistake?*
- *What would you do differently if you were in Rico's shoes?*

Table: Cheating vs. Honesty

Cheating Hurts	Honesty Helps
Hurts people around you	Builds trust with others
Causes stress and guilt	Creates relief and confidence
May result in punishment	Opens doors to second chances
Spreads unfairness	Earns respect and fairness

Real-Life Connection: Think about a moment when telling the truth was hard. How did you handle it? What could you do better next time?

🎯 ACTIVITY ZONE

ACTIVITY 1 – SENTENCE FIX-UP — TENSE DETECTIVE!

Read each sentence. Rewrite it correctly using the proper verb tense.

1. Rico copy Ana's test yesterday.
2. Ms. Lopez give the test today.
3. Ana look upset last week.
4. They studies for math now.
5. Rico cheat before, but now he learn.

ACTIVITY 2 – FILL-IN-THE-BLANK: FIX THE TENSE!

Fill in each sentence with the correct verb form based on the time clue.

1. Rico ____ for the test last night. (Past)
2. Ana ____ happy now. (Present)
3. Rico ____ on the test yesterday. (Past)
4. Ms. Lopez ____ strict today. (Present)
5. They ____ hard last week. (Past)

ACTIVITY 3 – CHEATING SCENARIO PICKER

Choose the best action for each situation below:

1) You're struggling with a test.
a) Copy a friend's answers
b) Ask for help before the test
c) Skip the test
d) Guess randomly
e) Do nothing

2) You see someone cheating.
a) Tell everyone
b) Talk to the teacher privately
c) Help them cheat
d) Ignore it
e) Copy them

3) You cheated and got caught.
a) Lie about it
b) Admit you were wrong
c) Blame someone else
d) Run away
e) Laugh it off

4) You're tempted to cheat on homework.
a) Copy from the internet
b) Study with a friend
c) Skip it
d) Make up answers
e) Pretend you did it

5) Your friend wants you to help them cheat.
a) Help them
b) Say no and offer to study together
c) Tell the teacher
d) Ignore them
e) Spread a rumor

ACTIVITY 4 –REFLECTION QUIZ — CHOOSE HONESTY!

Answer these questions based on what you learned in the story.

1) Why does honesty win?
a) It gets you in trouble
b) It builds trust
c) It's hard
d) It makes you famous
e) It's boring

2) Why did Rico cheat?
a) He studied too much
b) He didn't study
c) He liked math
d) He wanted an A
e) He was bored

3) How can you make things right after cheating?
a) Lie more
b) Admit it and fix it
c) Ignore it
d) Blame others
e) Cheat again

4) How did Rico feel after admitting he cheated?
a) Sad
b) Proud
c) Angry
d) Scared
e) Bored

5) Why did Ana thank Rico?
a) He got an A
b) He told the truth
c) He cheated again
d) He ignored her
e) He left class

ANSWERS
🎯 ACTIVITY ZONE

ACTIVITY 1 – SENTENCE FIX-UP — TENSE DETECTIVE!

1. Rico copied Ana's test yesterday.
2. Ms. Lopez gives the test today.
3. Ana looked upset last week.
4. They study for math now.
5. Rico cheated before, but now he learns.

ACTIVITY 2 – FILL-IN-THE-BLANK: FIX THE TENSE!

1. Rico **studied** for the test last night.
2. Ana **is** happy now.
3. Rico **cheated** on the test yesterday.
4. Ms. Lopez **is** strict today.
5. They **studied** hard last week.

ACTIVITY 3 –CHEATING SCENARIO PICKER

1. b) Ask for help before the test
2. b) Talk to the teacher privately
3. b) Admit you were wrong
4. b) Study with a friend
5. b) Say no and offer to study together

ACTIVITY 4 –REFLECTION QUIZ — CHOOSE HONESTY!

b) It builds trust
b) He didn't study
b) Admit it and fix it
b) Proud
b) He told the truth

Chapter 10 : UNFOLLOW ME

BLOCK TOXIC JADE

Braffic zetimo !!j

CHAPTER 10 –UNFOLLOW ME

What happens when a friend brings you down instead of lifting you up?

Learning Objectives:

- ☑ I can explain how to identify and let go of a toxic friendship.
- ☑ I can correctly use "it's" and "its" in writing.
- ☑ I can reflect on what makes a healthy friendship.
- ☑ I can apply contraction rules to make my writing clearer.

STORY —Breaking Free

Sofia's Stand

Sofia and Jade were close. They texted all day. But Jade was bossy. "Wear this," Jade said, pointing to Sofia's outfit. "Your style's lame." Sofia laughed it off, but it hurt. Jade always decided what they did. If Sofia said no, Jade got mad. "You're boring," Jade would text.

One day, Jade wanted Sofia to skip class. "Come hang out," Jade said. Sofia shook her head. "I can't. I have a test." Jade rolled her eyes. "You're no fun," she texted. She sent mean memes about Sofia to their group chat. Everyone saw. Sofia's stomach twisted.

At lunch, Sofia sat alone. Her friend Leo noticed. "Why's Jade so mean to you?" he asked. Sofia sighed. "She's my friend. I guess that's how she is." Leo frowned. "Real friends don't act like that."

Sofia thought about it. Jade's words made her feel small. She didn't like who she was with Jade. That night, Sofia texted her. "I need a break," she wrote. "Your texts hurt me." Jade replied, "Whatever. You're weak." Sofia blocked her.

The next day, Sofia hung out with Leo. He was kind. "You're cool just as you are," he said. Sofia smiled. She felt free. Dropping Jade was hard, but it gave her confidence.

Mind Map: Sofia's Friendship Trail

```
Toxic Friendship
├── Problem: Jade's manipulative
│   ├── Bosses Sofia
│   └── Sends mean texts
├── Result: Sofia feels bad
│   ├── Feels small
│   └── Sits alone
├── Turning Point: Sofia speaks up
│   ├── Talks to Leo
│   └── Texts Jade
└── Outcome: Breaks free
    ├── Blocks Jade
    ├── Hangs with Leo
    └── Feels confident
```

Why This Story Matters: Sofia's story shows that sometimes you have to let go to grow. Toxic friends hold you back. Real ones help you shine.

Grammar Focus — Mastering Contractions

What Are Contractions?

Contractions are shortened word forms that make writing and speech faster and more casual.

- It's = "it is" or "it has" → It's time to leave.
- Its = shows ownership → The dog lost its toy.

How to Use Them

- Use it's when you mean it is or it has.
- Use its when something belongs to "it."

Table: "It's vs. Its — Text It Right!"

Toxic Friends	Good Friends
Put you down	Lift you up
Boss you around	Respect your choices
Make you feel small	Make you feel strong
Hurt your confidence	Build your trust

Practice Example

Text: Its hard to block a friend.
Fix: It's hard to block a friend.
Why: "It is hard" → Use "it's."

Visual: Contraction Decision Tree

```
Need It's or Its?
    ├── Mean "it is" or "it has"?
    │    ├── Yes → Use it's
    │    └── No → Show possession?
    │         └── Yes → Use its
    └── Not sure? Say the full version to test.
```

Why This Helps: Clear texts show your meaning. Using the right form makes your messages sharp and smart.

REAL TALK — SPOTTING TOXIC FRIENDS

Discussion Questions

- How do you know when a friend is toxic?
- What made Sofia realize she had to walk away?
- What does a healthy friendship look like?

- Why do some people stay in hurtful friendships?
- How can you find friends who lift you up?

Table: Friendship Check

Cheating Hurts	Honesty Helps
Hurts people around you	Builds trust with others
Causes stress and guilt	Creates relief and confidence
May result in punishment	Opens doors to second chances
Spreads unfairness	Earns respect and fairness

Real-Life Connection: Think about a moment when telling the truth was hard. How did you handle it? What could you do better next time?

🎯 ACTIVITY ZONE

ACTIVITY 1 – SENTENCE FIX-UP — SPOT THE MISTAKE!

Rewrite each sentence using the correct form of "it's" or "its."

1. Its a tough day for Sofia.
2. The phone broke it's screen.
3. Its not easy to say no.
4. Jade's laptop lost it's battery.
5. Its been a long week.

ACTIVITY 2 – FILL-IN-THE-BLANK — CHOOSE THE RIGHT ONE!

1. ___ hard to lose a friend. (Means "it is")
2. The phone lost ___ signal. (Shows possession)
3. ___ a mean text from Jade. (Means "it is")
4. The app crashed on ___ own. (Shows possession)
5. ___ been a good day with Leo. (Means "it has")

ACTIVITY 3 – FRIENDSHIP SCENARIO PICKER

Choose the best action for each situation:

1. Your friend always tells you what to do.
2. A friend sends you mean texts.
3. You feel bad around a friend.
4. Your friend puts you down in a group chat.
5. You want to find better friends.

 ACTIVITY ZONE

ACTIVITY 4 –REFLECTION QUIZ — CHOOSE YOUR FRIENDS

1. How do you know a friend's toxic?
2. Why did Sofia stay with Jade at first?
3. When should you walk away from a friend?
4. How did Sofia feel after blocking Jade?
5. Why did Sofia text Jade about needing a break?

Please let us know how we're doing by leaving us a review.

ANSWERS
ACTIVITY ZONE

ACTIVITY 1 – SENTENCE FIX-UP — SPOT THE MISTAKE!

1. It's a tough day for Sofia.
2. The phone broke its screen.
3. It's not easy to say no.
4. Jade's laptop lost its battery.
5. It's been a long week.

ACTIVITY 2 – FILL-IN-THE-BLANK — CHOOSE THE RIGHT ONE!

1. It's
2. its
3. It's
4. its
5. It's

ACTIVITY 3 – FRIENDSHIP SCENARIO PICKER

1. b) Talk to them about it
2. b) Tell them it hurts you
3. b) Take a break from them
4. b) Leave the chat and talk to them
5. b) Join a club to meet kind people

ACTIVITY 4 – REFLECTION QUIZ — CHOOSE YOUR FRIENDS

1. b) They make you feel bad
2. b) They were close friends
3. b) They hurt you a lot
4. c) Free
5. b) To be honest about her feelings

conclusion

It Awing low!

CONCLUSION — YOU FINISHED! NOW WHAT?

🎉 Celebrate the Win

You did it!

You just read 10 powerful short stories packed with real-life drama, relatable characters, and grammar tips that didn't feel like homework. Whether you're in an IEP program, an ESL learner, or someone who thought reading wasn't your thing, this book proved otherwise.

Each chapter built your confidence, sharpened your grammar, and helped you think deeply about the choices teens face every day.

You didn't just read. You leveled up.

📚 What You Learned

Throughout this journey, you:

✅ Understood peer pressure, digital drama, and toxic friendships

✅ Learned how to fix sentence fragments, use quotation marks, and master contractions

✅ Practiced writing in real-world formats like texts, DMs, and dialogues

✅ Developed social-emotional awareness alongside grammar skills

✅ Realized that short stories + short sentences = real reading success
Reading is a muscle. You just flexed it ten times over.

Final Pep Talk

You may have started this book thinking,

"I'm not a strong reader."
But look at you now.

You've read real stories. Fixed real grammar. Faced real choices.
That's what a strong reader does.

You're not behind.

You're just getting started with the right kind of book.

So don't stop here. Keep reading. Keep writing.

And remember: reading your way still counts.

Thanks for reading.

You made it matter.

See you in the next book.

Appendix

APPENDIX -A : GRAMMAR HACKS CHEAT SHEET

📚 Grammar Problem	✖ Wrong Example	✅ Right Fix	💬 Text Tip 📱
Sentence Fragment	Running late.	I'm running late.	Finish your thought!
Commas in Dialogue	I'm done she said.	"I'm done," she said.	Comma before quotes!
Run-On Sentence	I'm late I ran.	I'm late. I ran.	Split it into two!
Homophones	Your late!	You're late!	"You're" = you are.
Subject-Verb Agreement	The team run fast.	The team runs fast.	"Team" needs "runs."
Pronouns	Mia lied. He's mad.	Mia lied. She's mad.	Match pronoun to person.
Quotation Marks	Mia said I'm sorry.	Mia said, "I'm sorry."	Quote exact words!
Verb Tenses	I study yesterday.	I studied yesterday.	"Yesterday" means past.
Contractions	Its my phone.	It's my phone.	"It's" = it is.

APPENDIX -B : READING LIKE A PRO – MINDMAP STRATEGY

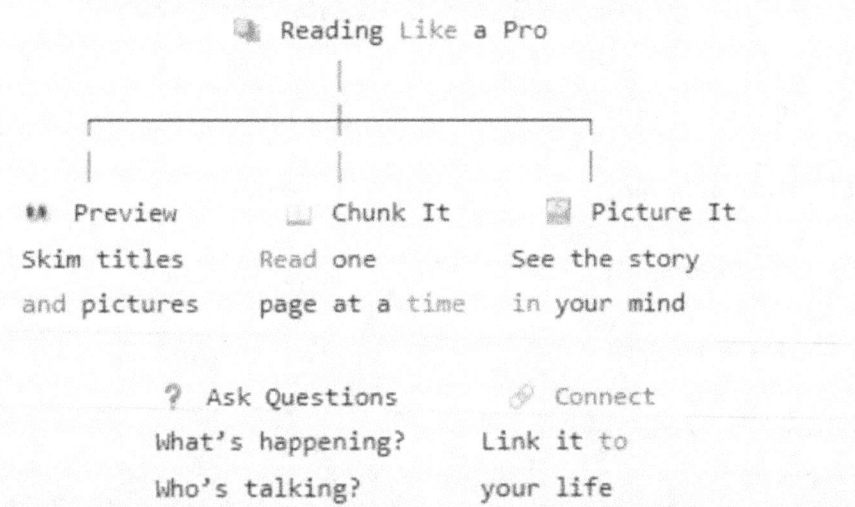

98

APPENDIX -C :
FIX YOUR WRITING – FLOWCHART STRATEGY

Purpose: Use this quick check flowchart before you hit "Send" on a message—or turn in your schoolwork. It catches common writing problems like fragments, run-ons, homophones, and more.

● Is my sentence clear?
├── ✅ YES → Good to go!
│   └── Example: "I'm ready now."
└── ❌ NO → Let's fix it:
    ├── ❓ Fragment? (Incomplete)
    │   ├── Fix: Add subject or verb
    │   └── Example: "Because I ran" → "I ran because I was late."
    ├── ❗ Run-On? (Too long)
    │   ├── Fix: Break into two sentences
    │   └── Example: "I'm late I ran" → "I'm late. I ran."
    ├── 🔄 Homophone? (Wrong word)
    │   ├── Fix: Use the correct word
    │   └── Example: "Your late" → "You're late."
    ├── ⏳ Verb Tense? (Wrong time)
    │   ├── Fix: Match past/present
    │   └── Example: "I study yesterday" → "I studied yesterday."
    └── ✂ Contraction Error? (It's vs. Its)
        ├── Fix: Test by saying "it is"
        └── Example: "Its cool" → "It's cool."

APPENDIX - D :
LIFE LESSONS VENN DIAGRAM

Book Lessons 📖 (Ch. 2–10)	**My Life** 💭 (Your Experiences)
Peer pressure *(Chapter 2)*	I lied to fit in
Gossip hurts *(Chapter 8)*	I heard a rumor
Honesty wins *(Chapter 9)*	I told the truth
Toxic friends *(Chapter 10)*	I ignored a bully

APPENDIX - E :
COMMON VOCABULARY MISTAKES (AND WHAT TO SAY INSTEAD)

✘ Confusing Word	✅ Say This Instead	🧠 Meaning / Tip
Affect	Change	"The post *changed* my mood."
Effect	Result	"The *result* was hurt feelings."
Accept	Say yes	"I *accepted* her apology."
Except	Not this one	"Everyone *except* Mia was there."
Their	Belongs to them	"It's *their* choice."
There	That place	"Let's go *there* now."
They're	They are	"*They're* going to the park."
Then	Time (next)	"We ate lunch, *then* left."
Than	Comparison	"He's taller *than* me."
Lose	Misplace	"Don't *lose* your phone."
Loose	Not tight	"My laces are *loose*."

APPENDIX - F :
MOST COMMON GRAMMAR GOOFS (AND HOW TO FIX THEM)

❌ Mistake	✅ Correction	💬 Quick Fix Tip
"Its raining outside."	"It's raining outside."	"It's" = it is
"There going home now."	"They're going home now."	"They're" = they are
"I seen that movie."	"I saw that movie."	Past tense of see = saw
"Him and me are friends."	"He and I are friends."	Subject = He/I (not Him/Me)
"The team are winning."	"The team is winning."	Team = one group → use singular
"I don't got no pencils."	"I don't have any pencils."	Avoid double negatives
"She don't like it."	"She doesn't like it."	He/She/It → use "doesn't"
"Me and Jay went to school."	"Jay and I went to school."	Always say "I" after others

APPENDIX - G :
TEXT SLANG VS. SCHOOL WRITING

📱 Text Slang	✏️ School Version	📌 When to Use
u	you	Only in texting
b4	before	Use full word in assignments
lol	(write how you feel)	Say "That was funny" in essays
idk	I don't know	Use full sentence when formal
cuz / bc	because	Always write "because" at school
gonna / wanna	going to / want to	Use full words in writing
thx	thanks	Use "thank you" in formal notes

APPENDIX - H:
CAPITALIZATION RULES MADE EASY

✓ Checkpoint	🔍 What to Look For	☑ Example
1. Capital letters?	Sentence starts with uppercase	"I love reading."
2. Punctuation?	Ends in a period, question mark, or exclamation	"Where are you going?"
3. Complete sentence?	Has subject + verb	"He runs fast."
4. Spelling mistakes?	No texting spellings	"Because" not "bc"
5. Makes sense aloud?	Read it out loud – does it flow?	"She said she was sorry."

APPENDIX - I:
QUICK FIX FOR RUN-ON SENTENCES

✗ Run-On Sentence	☑ Fixed Version	🔧 Fix Tip
"I was late I ran to school."	"I was late. I ran to school."	Use a period between ideas
"She yelled he ignored her."	"She yelled, and he ignored her."	Use a comma + conjunction
"We were hungry we ate pizza."	"We were hungry, so we ate pizza."	Break with 'so,' 'and,' or period
"They left I stayed behind."	"They left. I stayed behind."	Split two subjects with punctuation
"I texted he didn't answer."	"I texted, but he didn't answer."	Add 'but' with a comma

APPENDIX - J:
10 WORDS THAT OFTEN CONFUSE TEENS

🐻 Tricky Word	🗣 What It Means	☑ Sample Sentence
Compliment	A nice thing you say	"She gave me a compliment."
Complement	Something that goes well	"The shoes complement the dress."
Desert	Hot, sandy place	"Camels live in the desert."
Dessert	Sweet treat	"I love chocolate dessert."
Principal	School leader	"Our principal gave a speech."
Principle	A rule or belief	"That's a strong principle."
Stationary	Not moving	"The car was stationary."
Stationery	Paper and pens	"She bought new stationery."
To	Direction or action	"I went to the mall."
Too	Also / very	"I'm too tired today."

APPENDIX - K :
10 FAST GRAMMAR REMINDERS

These quick grammar tips will help you sound clear, confident, and correct, whether writing an essay or sending a text.

☑ **Complete your thoughts.**
Avoid sentence fragments like "Because I was late." → Finish it: "I was late because I overslept."

☑ **Use commas in dialogue.**
"I'm done," she said. (Not "I'm done she said.")

☑ **Don't mash sentences together.**
Break up run-ons: "He ran I followed." → "He ran. I followed."

☑ **Know your homophones.**
"Your cool" ✗ → "You're cool" ☑

☑ **Match subjects with verbs.**
"They goes" ✗ → "They go" ☑

☑ **Pick the right pronoun.**
"Mia said he lied." → Who's "he"? Be clear.

☑ **Use quotation marks for exact speech.**
Mia said, "I'm sorry."

☑ **Keep verb tense consistent.**
Don't switch between past and present unless needed.

☑ **Check contractions.**
"Its raining" ✗ → "It's raining" ☑

☑ **Read out loud like a DM.**
If it sounds awkward, it probably needs a fix.

APPENDIX - L :
10 READING TRICKS THAT ACTUALLY WORK

Use these simple strategies to make reading easier, less stressful, and way more fun.

- **Preview before reading.**
  Skim the title, pictures, and bold words.

- **Chunk it up.**
  Don't read everything at once—go paragraph by paragraph.

- **Picture it.**
  Visualize the scene in your head like a movie.

- **Ask questions as you go.**
  "Who is this about?" "What just happened?"

- **Make connections.**
  Relate the story to your own life, a friend, or something you've seen online.

- **Mark what's confusing.**
  Use a pencil, sticky note, or digital highlighter.

- **Talk about it with someone.**
  Saying it out loud builds understanding and confidence.

- **Summarize like a text.**
  "This story = she lied, got caught, felt bad."

- **Pause and predict.**
  Guess what will happen next to stay involved.

- **Celebrate small wins.**
  Read one page? That counts. Understanding one sentence? That's progress.

YOUNG WRITER SERIES - DR. FANATOMY

Please let us know how we're doing by leaving us a review.

www.ingramcontent.com/pod-product-compliance
Lightning Source LLC
Chambersburg PA
CBHW081402070526
44583CB00020B/2648